A WANDERING PEN

POEMS

BY

F.J.Milne

Poems

Preface

A book of 100 poems. An eclectic mix of
reflective poetry. The Theme is LIFE.

As a very ordinary person who is compelled to
write at any opportunity, I observe life in all its
glorious colours.
Some of these poems are bright and joyful
whilst others have a paler shade, touched by the
challenges of everyday.

My writing is mostly inspired by others, who
unknowingly trip that switch of creativity and
allow my pen to express itself with emotion
using simple words.

I choose to be uncomplicated, ordinary, a few
words on a page can feed the soul.

CONTENTS

Flamboyant Attire

Take a glimpse a glance as you pass on by

Don't be fooled by that extraordinary attire

It's there for show to catch a moment

A blink in time

Don't be fooled again by that

Flamboyant attire!

So Many Things

There are so many things to write about
in the skip of a beat, or glimpse of the eye.
A snap of wonder as it trundles by.

There are so many things of magnificence
from a simple pebble to a mountain high.
A creation so small to the naked eye with its
tiny perfection as the world goes by.

Attentive moments trip the switch
as colours flash – yet fade and dim
if not recaptured through a wandering pen.

A Lifetime of Words

A lifetime of words

leaves so much to spare

the thoughts that flash by

between the now and the where.

Imagine a day when all becomes

clear those words full to exploding

bursting forth on the air.

Vibrations capturing every ear

to listen, to hear the melody,

the rhythm, the pulse and the beat,

then the silence

the hush as words slowly creep

to nestle in minds and

safely keep for ever.

A lifetime of words is never enough!

Memory

I love a story

The yarn that's spun

The words that stir a memory

The expression in the eyes

As they look far away

Living in that moment

That was once a yesterday.

Colourful People

So many faces, smiles, meeting eyes.

So many chatting mouths, sipping lips.

So many nodding heads, shaking hair.

So many feet, still or moving, holds the beat.

So many people engaged in their own

and other people's lives.

So many words to write to paint

this scene of colourful people.

So many, too many - so I'll

just linger and look!

Layers

To be wrapped and enwrapped
layer upon layer from the softest
delicate to the intricate flair.

Layer upon layer forms a secret
cocoon where only the outside
is seen as the view.

Each minute each moment
adds to the veil that hides the
real stories too many to tell.

The time is just waiting
one day unannounced the
cocoon will unravel
 in a magnificent flounce
Just wait!

That Story

There is that story to tell
that wanders around stirring dust
from distant past or beams into
present day.

That story needing to be told
to any listener on park bench or bus
stop queue to anyone with
time to stay.

Words that flutter as butterflies
released one summer's day to land
on strangers newly met just pass the
time of day.

So tell that story spare no ears, no words,
no tears.
So tell that story, tell it with no fear but hear
it's echo carried on.

Blending

Low lights shimmer in the misty scene,
music beats and pulses in the mellow fog.
Relaxed and cool, demanding nothing,
compelling something yet unknown.

Spinning thoughts, vibes unchallenged,
free to wander.
Bitter taste over lips already tainted
with ruby wine.

Solitude bites into late night blues,
so alone.
Voices remote, lull, not intruding this
blending union.

Pen flows unthinking, expressing only
what it feels unheeded.
Feelings flow through pens ability to know.

Autumn Scene

Slipping past my window, late

sun brightening October's scene,

lighting up autumnal skies.

Trees holding on their beauteous

dress so soon to fall.

Colours of such varied hues from

golden yellow to deepest red.

Such glorious views to brighten days

before the winter gloom.

With calm that rests before the sleep,

a peaceful space to reap and

treasure nature's best when all will slide

into quiet arrest and freeze in expectation.

The icy frost all glistening pure

will greet its chilling counterpart as

biting winds fly o'er the land.

We wait for bud and blossom!

Just sitting

Silence
shouts with every noise
stillness
rushes by
eyes wide open
blankly stare
at nothing
calmness
rocks in restless storm
tranquillity
churns with turbulent spawn
in a jungle crowd
solitude
is just sitting.

Art in Progress

The cupboards embrace their tumble.
The cushions are squashed to shape
they fit the dog and everyone
a work of art to make.
The dishes in tottering towers
just teeter on the brink of
transforming each encrusted plate
into a gaudy new mosaic.
Papers strewn half open
relax with part read news
draping tabletops or chair arms
printed collage in the room.
Mirror's hazy lustre with no sparkle
and no shine reflects those misty images
of comfort in design.
The exhibit as contemporary shows
living modern style with unmade beds
and scattered clothes a tapestry of life it grows
in colour rich and plenty.

Minimalistic

A clutter, a clutch or jumble,

a lot, a little or few.

Too much, not enough, too many,

are the words that explain what we store.

Eclectic, modern, minimalistic,

retro, antique or bizarre,

are words that are used without conscience

to explain what we manage to store.

We say "Let's have a good clear out"

but find empty space such a bore.

Now *tha*t you see is the problem

so it's off to gather lots more!

Dusting the Dog

He's curled up on the sofa
Half chewed bone buried deep
They say that it's a dog's life
But all he does is sleep

Eyes follow every movement
To the kitchen when I cook
Hoping that it's dinner time
He gives that doggy look

His tail beats out a rhythm
That says he's so content
No matter how I tell him "OFF"
My energy's misspent

I've warned him I'll be cleaning
He just wags his waggy tail
'till he sees that yellow duster
Then his whole world starts to pale.

Tap a Tempo

Garble and nonsense
rolls off the tongue
titillates the eardrums
exercise the lungs
rattle through the rhythms
let the words flow
who cares what they mean
just let them all go.

Roll on every riddle
tongue tied up in knots
there's joy in endless twaddle
until the babbling stops
feet dance until they're dizzy
lips smile to show delight
voices chant in raucous unison or
shout with all their might.

Everybody does it
but best when not alone
for clapping hands need hands to
clap the message that we own
the rhythm of life's within us all
to follow as we go without a glance
or backward stare it's simply
there to show.

From rocking cradle to the grave
its tempo has to flow.

A Dance in Leather Hide

I saw them in the window
they caught my passing glance
so neatly resting side by side
toes pointed as in dance.

I had to stop not pass them
and look most every day
would someone else just
snap them up and take them far away?

I began to call them "my shoes"
they simply were the best
for every time I saw them
they stood out from the rest.

I would not feel the pain they'd cause
instead my feet would glide
we'd dance along together
I'd wear them with such pride.

Bright shoes in dazzling leather
to keep my feet tight in
as I stepped along so lightly
I would try hard not to sing!

Foot Power

Feet are an absolute pain
you know they take you where *they* want
to go dragging you where you've never
been and getting lost.

I took mine out the other day
to stop and linger along the way
but then they started to complain
they'd had enough.

So I treated them to a shiny new
coat of leather in a shade of blue
they ached to show their
gratitude by puffing up with pride.

What am I going to do with you?
I asked my feet as if they knew
thankfully, there was no reply
but they'd had their say already.

Like a ball and chain they felt
like lead I wished for another
pair instead as I coaxed them home
reluctantly they had no choice
but to follow *me*!

Illusive

Gone in a flying sigh

a whisper, a flutter

just enough to catch an

eye or two.

Perhaps a distant view

to dance in shadows

silent as the morning dew

illusive.

Inner Space

To contemplate is necessary
to ruminate is a must
to meet that deeper thought
that comes to stay.

You hear all yet hear nothing
the body warms yet feels so cool
keep it close as the moment stays
for just a while.

Keep that inner space within
whilst the world just tumbles by.

Expansion

Warm to the bite

Dripping in such a decadent way

Gently giving to the mouth

No don't get carried away.

Soft and so inviting

Without any glamour at all

It simply can't be beaten

In any shape or form.

Comforting for the moment

Whether morning, noon or night

There's no right time to indulge this

It all depends on you.

It's downright pure temptation

Confront it with no dread

Just dress it with your favourite

Perhaps jam or chocolate spread.

There is just one expansion

As the waistline slowly grows

All pleasure has its story

Like this breaded tale of woe!

Ragged and Frayed

It clung to the branch like a limp lost thing,
bedraggled, ragged and frayed.
Gusts had carried it far from its path
where it meant not to wander or stray.

With a flutter and swirl it flew high
in escape, but only to land in the gutter.
Held in the grip of a gurgling flow, where
all things end up as no matter.

Rain washed its face like tears in free flow,
blurring message so tenderly tendered.
True love never knew those words, precious
though few, that ended as simply just litter.

Just the Silence

I love the stillness of the night

no footstep, no bird song, no fox call

carried on the air.

Just the Silence.

I love the blackness of the night

no sun, no stars, no glint

or chink of light.

Just the Silence.

I feel the air upon my face

so fresh, so cool, drift in from

open casement.

I smell the rain about to fall

then pound, on ground, beating

out its message to a harsh

world.

Whilst I still love

the stillness of the night.

A Glimpse Under the Tree

We sit so very lightly as if
cushioned on a cloud
beneath the pinkest parasol
the world has ever found.

We talk yet all is silent
bird song keeps the moment true
nature offers many places
to keep company with you.

We sip tea from delicate cups
yours has angels round the rim
you say you cannot stay long
now it's near the end of spring.

We look up into the canopy
as petals start to fall
like brides dressed in pink confetti
we laugh at folly's fuel.

I raise my hand to brush them
those petals from your hair but
find that I am quite alone
you are no longer there.

We'll meet again in summer
under dappled shades of green
to breathe the freshest air
that there has ever been.

No Answer

If it were possible to glide on the surface
of life where only ripples caress the
  turbulence of emotion and thought.

If it were only possible to be still in
rocky seas to calmly ride those tossing
waves unruffled and unperturbed.

Would it all be just a blind disguise,
a false pretence,
a place to hide,
a dream, a wish?
When all is fire and rage and passion
  unspent.

Arrested

Heads bow in concentration

Fingers gliding-poking-tapping

Eyes focus glaringly transfixed

Sun glancing on faces sideways

Rain lashing in rivulets creep

Wind breaking crashing wildly

Buildings eyes upon the world

Trees branching strong and bold

Meadows cushioning sky blue sky

Bridges straddling silver grey

Gulls swooping flying sail on high

The scene calls for admiration

Yet technology arrests the eye!

Grey

She stood lonely yet not alone

a loyal friend tethered beside her.
She in her grey anorak he with his
grey whiskers.
Waiting
It was a grey day full of autumn
dampness.
One of those days that offers no ray
of sunshine.
She raised her hand to wave her
face brightened in a smile.
The dog stood patiently beside her
on long spindly legs with waggy tail.
She raised her hand to wave again
as the train pulled out her lips said
Goodbye!

Metronome

It's a challenge to be a part of this
ever changing world. Past is now
a history with many stories to be told.
Perhaps settling down to a gentler
kind of pace, would give more time to
savour each moment without haste.

Yet is it really difficult to be dignified
with grace, to keep the rules not break
them in a carefree kind of way?
The rhythmic voice of reason steadfast as always
says 'There's no real point in sticking to a
plan that's bound to sway.'

No rules should make the best rules
yet a balance must prevail, with a beat that's on
the upbeat the metronome ticks each day.
Slowly take a gentle step each footfall leaves
a trace, with imprints left behind you whatever
path you make.

Observations

There is a man sitting over there
with a shiny pate, no hair, glasses and a book.
He is adorning a yellow scarf draped
down his tweedy suit.
I can see he is just like me
thinking and watching carefully.

Scribbling in a small notebook
he stops now and then to look
and wait for the voice of inspiration.
He is comfortably seated as am I
in leather chairs best and most
desirable in this coffee shop.

I wonder what he is writing as I
write about him. He is inspired
as I can see yet he has caught my
attention and inspired me!

Lobby Hop

Back and forth go the pedestrians
heels a clicking under cover.
Doing the stroll or faster pace so
where's the race?

One or two, then a following few
caught up in the Lobby Hop.
A nonchalant amble step past in a pair,
now a busy bustler who wafts the air.
The engaging mobile wrapping an ear
around every bend and every staircase.
The catwalk strut is for the brave where
eyes that follow transfix to a glaze.

Ten thousand steps is no problem
when stepping up to the Lobby Hop.
I have to confess as a watcher it's
not my race!

Ordinary

It's just an ordinary day
In an ordinary way
No flying high to reach
The sky no floating by
On silvery stars.

It's precious to be ordinary
Looking out upon the
Extra ordinary world
Enclosed within a
Super ordinary bubble!

Something Beautiful

It takes your breath away
to leave suspended on the air
that drop of vapour for the
words you could not say.

Then steals your heart which
sometimes lost finds solace in
such tender care. A touch
between hot fire and soft embrace
falls gently on the senses
to land without a sound.

Yet asks for nothing in a
most magnificent way, but soothes
those slowly wilting edges so
shyly on display.

Never

I just wanted you to know me

I didn't want you to own me

Just to be a little closer

To smile to chill be someone

You said I was unusual

I think you were delusional

You should have kept your

Distance I told you not to care

Not to be a fool 'cause you didn't

Know me you will never be the man

The man that tells my story 'cause

You'll never own me

That's a wrap!

Haze

It's got to come from the heart
otherwise it's not worth the ink.
It's got to come from the heart
lest those words just slowly sink.
To capture on a page that cluster,
that haze of words, like birds in flight,
arrested for a moment yet just
wanting to fly free.

The break

uneasy ripples murmur
restlessly
stirring the stillness
under grey horizons

air heavy with intent
brooding
deep and dark
lulls before the break

the crack splits the silence
crashing
force and fury
send rumbles in its wake

turning churning chopping
with angry toss and tumble
lashing at the day

Enjoyment Trap

On the edge of sanity
caught in the enjoyment trap
where bottles dressed alluringly
stand upright behind the bar.

Ears throb to a pounding beat
eyes dilate where shadows creep
mind numbs and lulls
into slow retreat.

The curl of tongues as voices rise
are thick with curse and drink
gruff grunts and sighs hide
lonely eyes as spirits rise and sink.

The name etched out in letters
decorates the door to let
those fading eyes that pass
know they've been here before.

Passion's Sleep

Entangled webs we weave where thoughts
and passions tread to fill the heart with torrid
dreams.

Restless spirits toss and jest in an unreal
world.
Imagination conjures images so bright to fill
the heart with dread.

Bitter pain so deep it grips the soul as
daylight breaks to leave behind a yearning
hope to meet again in passion's sleep.

In the Dark

Stillness in the dark

Head restless on the pillow

Air mingles with the breath

Eyes seek a chink of light.

Thoughts bounce about confused

Plans plan in turbulent drifts

Music with no sound beats

Silently in the dark.

Patient

It's the waiting that gets you into
the waiting mode.

Mind searches corners to occupy
whilst eyes take in surroundings.
People in barren chairs of dullest blue
settle on floors of depressing hue.
Waiting for a name call or two
in the longest ever queue.

Good news or bad, mended or not
incurs patient patients to await
their slot!

Lost Instructions

I'm told they're so important
with numbers one to ten
of do's and don'ts to follow
in order, not mayhem.

But it's really tiresome trying
to remember what they are
so I've put them in the lost drawer
where they're better off by far.

Random and haphazard are
sometimes much more fun
with a sprinkling of forgetfulness
until the job is done.

What happened to spontaneous
he's not inside the drawer
but hiding with flamboyant
just outside the door.

I'll open doors and windows
to let the air flow free
without those lost instructions
it's far easier to be me!

Present Day

Used to do, be, or see
used to want, seek or look
beneath every tree, every place.

Never finding hide-a-ways or
lingering shady corners
of those used to be days.

Like passing shadows resting
just nestling memories
that brings light to the present day
and this moment!

Red

Red is my colour, it fires
passion in the blood.
It's bold and brave and opulent
I use it without dread.
From crimson to vermillion
the mix is so sublime
it enhances every colour
without it I would pine.

Red is my colour, it never
lets me down, from ruby lips
to sauce on chips it's there for
permanent time.
No I won't go down in purple
as lovely as it is,
I choose instead the brightest
of the fieriest of red.

Sanctuary

Brown visage aged and sagging
like years on a crumpled face
indents deep – now permanent –
say how you welcome those
who nestle there.

All shapes and sizes rest their buttocks
within your open arms
some round and plump go sinking low
whilst thinner ones find space to grow.

Your shiny leather like a smile
invites a resting place
where conversation prattles on – or –
whispers hold the space.

Hands stretch across broad arms
hot palms are your embrace
as elbows dig and furrow
you surrender with such grace.

To be the choice above all others
whose hard wood grinds with bone
you're a sanctuary island, a refuge –
a place like home.

Simplest Form

I don't wear rings on my fingers bows in my
hair.
I don't wear diamonds in my ears or strings
of silvery pearls.
No place for velvets or lace in softest drapes
and furls.
No silks and satins adorning this kind of girl.

Just wrap me in gentleness breathe your
breath with mine.
Just let myself be naked in a peaceful state of
mind.
To end at the beginning in simple state and
form.
No struggle no sound but the silence in a
storm.

Spreading the Word

I've tried to write this many times
as there's something I have to say.
It concerns me not a little bit
that it might just come your way.

When you're dressing in the
morning poised on one leg
or on two beware 'cause it's
invisible just waiting to catch you.
Perhaps you'll be walking down
the street on a calm or windy day
it's always lurking round about
with you it loves to play.

Feet capture its imagination
in heels or flats or bare
it can't resist a little fun so
a trip is always there.
A waver, wobble or a weave
say it's watching you close by
choosing inconvenient moments
to surprise you on the sly.

I've noticed it myself you see
so I want to spread the word
then you'll know it when it
wobbles by, you can say
'I've already heard.'

Sidelong Glance

And so it was that by and by
she stole a look.
A sidelong glance from the
corner of her eye.
There it was that invitation
that glinted out of reach.
Silence cornered her, closed
her in with a protective cloak,
shut her down.
It was that never forgotten
out of reach look!

Sound Waves

It's o.k. to say it
and say it again
but don't delete it
it's never the same

It's o.k. to say it but
never in vain for
flippant words just
cause pain

If you've already thought it
then think again before
words slip out lest
you cannot reclaim!

A Fresh Start

The wind came rattling at my door
I did not let it in.
I told it –
"Go, get out of here, find somewhere else to
spin."

I'll wait until a calmer day then
open just a chink
to see what's round the corner and
maybe then I'll think -

It's worth a venture forth today
the air is fresh as dew,
the rain has stopped, the sun is out
and I feel quite brand new.

Back of your Mind

Follow me I'll be behind you
listen to the words you'll hear.
Don't hurry on, don't rush or run,
take time to see what's real.

You go and test the waters first
tread gently in the mire.
Yet follow me I'll be behind you,
to nurture lest you fall.

Freedom flies with wings on high
it's no game of chance you play.
Follow me I'll be behind you,
let wisdom guide your way .

Those words of caution on the air
you didn't want to hear, now
gently nestle in your mind and always
will be near.

Stepping Through the Frame

Something about it made her eyes glisten
it caught her breath with unsaid words
it was part of her life, had moved with
her through many places.

I wondered how many times she had
stepped through the frame.

It was always there unnoticed, invisible to the
passing eye that saw no connection or emotion
as it hung looking down, inviting curious
eyes to be transfixed by its mystical charm.

I wondered how many times she had
stepped through the frame.

Her words caught me up unguarded, I felt the
pain around her heart, it told of longing and of
memories in a world she never shared.

Her secret world where no one else had ever dared.

I waited quietly for the invite as through
the frame I softly stepped.

The light had suddenly faded to a soft yet
magical hue of greens in beautiful palette
brushed mistily with a dash of blue. Boughs
arched above entwining, touching all within
their reach, shutting out the sky or any eye that
might be watching too.

The path beneath those silent feet was couched
in springy moss to leave no mark of any kind
left painted virgin new. Golden threads threaded
through the green, a simple light to light the scene,
a welcome warmth from the artists brush to say,
'Come in there is no rush in this quiet mystical world'.

She kept her secret to herself but shared a tiny glimpse.
I never knew what moved her so, through that frame of
misty hues.

Familiarity

Your eyes
like cameras
take
those first impressions
from morning's wake.

Familiar sights
in a familiar way.
How used they are to see
and yet
I wonder what they view.

No one knows excepting you
that words can never fully tell.

What colours
are they bright as new
or
faded in a haze of blue?

You look at me
I look at you -
we see the shell the outside view.
You think you know me
it can't be true.

I don't know myself
So how could you?

No Name

There is a place that has no name,

between a nightmare and a lover's dream.

Between the sun and tumbling rain,

between the hills and oceans wide.

There is a place that has no name.

Tranquil in a no name place,

it rarely ever shows its face.

It hides inside the outward stare,

it hides in minds that feel despair.

It is a place that has no name,

it hides between fear and shame.

Quiet and shadowy it has no name!

Fool or Not

An optimistic optimist rides on the back
of hope, sees through the murky shadows
without fear.

A pessimistic pessimist's companion
is despair, to traverse the mists of
hopelessness on a journey
never clear.

The question needs an answer though
impossible to say -
Is a pessimist a realist or an optimist
a fool?

Tell Yourself......

You're amazing, the words you hear so many
times now said with heartfelt praise.

How do you manage to be so kind when all
around challenges the human side?
To carry each day in a gentle way, unseen by
eyes that choose to turn away.
When all seems hopeless, dark and bitter,
you struggle back.
The pit that wrenches, drawing at your soul,
you shake it off.

You're amazing, much stronger than you think,
be proud to have an honest heart.

Just know that some who care so much would
hold you in their arms.
A bond that makes a difference to share
with all mankind. Courage is your strength.
Hope is your friend.

So tell yourself you're Amazing!

Time

Don't wait for me I'll catch you up
your pace I cannot take.
I need to stop make time stand still
not follow in your wake.

Just let me dream and think my thoughts
head high up in the clouds.
I'll linger longer days to years
don't lead me to your shrouds.

If you look back you'll see I'm gone
far out of sight and view.
I'll not be there when you reach the gates
my path is still too new.

Companion

Loneliness is a companion
it clasps a hand within
to tell its own sweet story
no matter how sparse or thin.

Loneliness never rushes it has
nowhere else to go it
stays close by to linger
with a painful empty flow.

Proud

She moved her arms so gently in the wind
as if conducting music to her own rhythm.

She stretched so high limbs lifted under
the air as if weightless.
Dressed in the darkest green, glistening
with the falling raindrops she stood
proud beneath the greyest sky.
A sudden gust tore at her majestic stance
now she groaned and tossed, its challenging
strength brought a look of ague.
She bent and strained, yet she
was not lost.

She stood proudly evergreen, whilst around
her barren sisters waited patiently.

Worry .... That's all

How fearsome life is a state of
being yet not being real.
Anxiety nestles between the good
and the unknown.
Will it be or will it not be the last kiss
the last caress?
How delicate the balance walking on
a tight rope of fear.
What is there to be sure about,
to rejoice and celebrate without that
twinge lurking in the belly.
Life is given in a cry of breath, taken
with a fading sigh.
The in between is laced with passion
red, moody blue, yellow bright as a
sunny hue, starry nights, rapid
storms, ever changing challenges
like tiny spores waiting to land
uninvited. That's all!

The Dreamer

Reality is never real, it spikes between
a distant dream, it pokes around in an easy
way becomes emerged in a ceaseless scheme.

Reality is how you see the world today
within your eye, for now it is what you ask of
it, to blur the edges delicately.

Reality has the softest touch, misted in
a haze as such, so do not to let it interfere,
for now reality just breeds fear.

Something or Nothing

is nothing emptiness
a void to be filled
in a moment of calm
as the heartbeat stills
is nothing something
looking for a space
awaiting an invite
with elegance and grace
is nothing peaceful
a time without haste
holding expectations in
a quiet embrace
is nothing secretly
misted in disguise
revealing itself in everything
to recognition's eyes?

A Buddha's Wink

Beneath the clouds there is a stillness. Gentle
breeze that hardly holds a movement yet
sways the tops of highest trees.

There is a stillness, healing quiet that lets
thoughts roam and stir in those dark corners;
where loneliness and desolation finds a secret
place to hide.
Time to think what has gone before and gives
today a different hue.
The struggle that appears to be overcome but
rears up to greet the morning when self is the
discovery of the day.
Peaceful space to strengthen soul and revalue
what is real, to gracefully balance this restless
spirit of today.

I think that Buddha just winked at me!
There is so much to see and hear in this
peaceful zone. Even on a sunless day there is
a blanket warm.
Deciding where to go and what to do with
time as it moves on. Sitting contemplating
does not produce the answer in itself but
reassures to calm that inner doubt.

In this beautiful space I reach for my pen as
always it seems to wander in a knowing way.
It shows me wisdom sometimes lost along the
way.

Now I am sure that Buddha winked at me!
Peacefully.

Top Gear

I've taken to wearing hats!

Berets with pom poms, velvets or straw,

I can't get enough I long for some more.

Woolly and soft or feathery with plumes,

ear flaps for lugs that hate winter's gloom.

Animal print or a furry festoon, crushing

the brow or topping my mop.

Turbans and tassels, snoods or peaked caps,

toories and tartan a rainbow of hats.

Oh look! Pointy fingers, a giggle, a stare.

Can't you see I don't mind, I really don't care

'cause I've taken to wearing hats!

Definition

Love is an easy word to say,
its meaning holds the answer
of feelings left to stray.

It's tears and smiles and a soft embrace.
It's pain and joy and a sinking heart.
It's sleepless nights and a hopeless state.
It's thoughts and dreams and a calmer space.

It's all one gives straight from the heart,
to those who matter.

Yet
Love is not an easy word to know.

Rain Wandering

She wandered as the rain
spotted her face, chilled her
down, made her steps heavy
and cumbersome.

There was no sign or recognition
of any familiar place among the
throngs bustling on wet pavements.
People bumped and buffeted as
they passed almost as if she had
no right to be among them.

She heard voices close behind her
as anxious steps closed in on the
narrow pavement. She stopped,
turned to look, stepped aside with
caution, lest she trip on curb or
gutter, to let them pass.

Smiles and conversation, ensued
amusing and engaging.
How easy a few words en-passant can
be with complete strangers.

And she was one of them!

Take a Look

Today I say you're too good to waste
don't walk in the shadow of others
who cast that cloud.
Take a look and see who you really are,
who you can be, without that cloud of fear
and tears carried heavy in your heart.

You are loved by those who truly love you
yet to linger in the past is fool's own tragedy.
Take a look and see who you really are,
take a step into the bright light, be kind
to yourself perhaps you will glow with the
light of hope.

Absorb the rays that will lift you to a better
place
leave that cloud behind you!

A Soft Touch

Don't wear black for me

I wear enough blackness for everyone else

Don't wear that sad face for me

I wear enough sadness to fill ample space

Red orange yellow or blue

Floppy hats floaty scarves and a flower or two

Neat neck ties adjusted just right

Now pretend we can swirl and twirl

All night

So smile with your lips

With your heart with your eyes

And remember that colour you see

In the skies

It's all in the rainbow or lines

Every cloud

Bluest blue yonder sprinkled starry

Night skies

Soft touch on a whispering breeze

Remember to wear your colours for me!

Time's Game

Time either goes so fast
or too slow for comfort.
Tumbling, rolling at its pace
it barely stops as in a race
that has no winner.
The past becomes more distant
faded in a dream of fantasy.
It is more difficult to recognise
what once was a reality.

When the rushing slows to a sedate
pace with steps that falter,
images that drift between
night and day, inviting constant slumber.

It plays a game, now no one cares called….
'Too Slow for Comfort.'

So Wait a While

Shall we meet in darkest night
under starry skies where soft feet
float on crystal tread.
Shall we meet on brightest day
in fields of corn where golden light
over us adorn.
Perhaps to sail on oceans blue
and rock beneath a cloudless sky.
Perhaps to sit on tufts of green
surrounded by a wondrous scene.
I see you with your softest look
in every place and every nook.
You fill my space, my heart, my soul
in night or day.
You must know now you didn't go
to leave me on my very own.

So wait a while I'll catch you there
under lamp lights golden glow.

The Fall

…..and here it comes again.…

That glitch, that unexpected moment.
That crunch, that hard place looming.

As if floating in an unreal time, slow
motion, yet unable to arrest its ultimate end.

Hard landing inevitable, mind saying
'Here it comes again' that hard place
looming!

Waiting

So restlessly she waits, passing traffic lulls
and rumbles into her silent mind.

She touches her hair with fidgety fingers,
adjusts her dress. The mind calms but
the hands move around hither and thither
adjusting, then readjusting, unable to be still.
She looks towards the door, her eyes linger
for a moment, so restlessly she waits.
Was that a step approaching or just
the stealthy creak of polished boards?
 She wonders if she should suddenly run
out of the door, down the steps and away
like the wind, so nobody would notice or
hear her rush of breath.

The door creaks slowly open
now she knows it's simply too late!

A Thousand Stories

It's there, barely audible,
that breath to let it out,
yet keep it all locked away.
It says no words but
tells a thousand stories.
Revealing nothing to the
cheek that feels it,
or the air that absorbs it,
or the frost that shows it,
 or the eyes that turn to look.
It reveals nothing.
Is it sheer delight,
or secret flight on a rainy day?
Is it memories of happy times,
or loss and loneliness?
Yet it tells a thousand stories
to the one who holds that breath
of a sigh.

A Capable Woman

She's full of wordy moments,
you see passion in her eyes. She
breathes her strength around you
to raise your head up high.

She's a rock a solid lean on
to catch your tumble or fall.
Yes, a capable woman
expects to manage it all!

She lifts you on those grey days
when the world seems bitter and sour.
When you can't see an end to the
turmoil, when you're lost in a milieu crowd.

With her heart weighed down and heavy
it soars again with hope.
Yet there's a question left to ask her –
Is a capable woman ever not able to cope?

Station Watch

Colourful flags to watch
as drifters drift to
who knows where.
A sea of faces shades
of pale or more exotic hues.

Some feet showing toes whilst
others wrestle so enclosed.
Family's clutch their young lest
they get lost in wander.

Baggage bumps and jolts
to trip or bruise a criss
cross cruiser.
Stress shows on frowning faces.

Departure times click slowly on
inviting constant toing and froing.
But me oblivious to time or travel
just sit and watch –

this parade of flags in colour!

Poetry

I love the words that mix with my head

I love the way they flow on the page

The colours the shadows the shade

Like a flower with no roots

Petals drift in the wind to

Settle in patterns of rhythm and rhyme

I love the pen that scratches and scrawls

But most of all

I like the end when those words have all been

spent!

Tell Me

When is it time to be ones true self
is there ever an appropriate spot?
Convention holds claws and
a tight tight knot that
hinders fetters and restrains.

If I were a real me I'd walk
naked you see with a notepad tied
to my hips to catch all those thoughts
in a colourful frame then dress
every tree like a fluttering vane.

I'd wander around free spirit I'd
found and do whatever I want
no harm to no man nor beast
is my plan but they'd lock me up
as a crank!

Coda

There are no words

Written or unsaid

To fill the void

The silence of my lips

My pen that rests

For now no utterance

Would suffice

All was carried with you

When you left.

The Long Marriage

If only the disturbed clatter
the panic and the words
said in frustration
didn't matter.

I hear you from a distance
the sounds penetrate my calmer
place. I prefer to remain
detached. I choose not to come
to your aid.

It's happened before, I don't know
how many times.
Behind closed doors I exercise restraint.
I thought perhaps you'd manage
you've been training for so many years.
Combustion takes control, aromas
drift with bitter note. I hear you shout,
"I've burnt the toast again!"

Work it...

It just works like this
it only takes a moment
a pause, a thought, a breath.

It simply works like that
a drop in the ocean, a speck
in the sky, a simple moment.

It always works for those
who give a moment, who
take a chance to stop.

Whisper

Words that crush the heart or lift the spirit
Words left unsaid for fear of saying
Words never telling how much is said.

Words too many to share caught
In death's own whisper.

Tomorrow is our Day

Tomorrow is the day to drift and
stray.
To feel the earth so cool beneath
our feet.
To run like wild things carried on
the wind.
To catch at floating sun beams
never caught.
To jostle under rain drops softest
fall.
Tomorrow is our day to slip the
leash and greet each morn anew
with patient grace.
For tomorrow never comes they
say.
So wait until tomorrow becomes
Today!

The Hubbub

This is what I love the hub and the bub

The background of voices blending

The clink and hiss and clatter

The busyness and relaxation

The shall I go or shall I stay

The writing in the corner

The watching the world go by

The feeling of invisibility

The jazz that suddenly hits the soul

This is why I'm here!

Soon

Let's walk together down narrow lanes
I'll hold your hand if you hold mine

Let's smile at faces as they smile back free
from covid's disguise.

Let's remember the past that is gone
For the future is lurking unclear.

The shade of an unfamiliar hue will rise
When can we breathe again.

A Question

When does a beginning
begin to begin
how does it know it's begun
does it meet itself
on its spiralling way and
turn into another one
if the beginning's the start
with no end to the flow
then is there ever a
beginning to know?

Inside or Out

smooth cool no line or crack
to let the inside out
or perhaps to keep
the outside out as well
if the inside stays where
it ought to be
the image remains intact
but one sharp tap and
all is revealed
like marshmallow in a
chocolate trap!

Comfort Zone

I'm torn between
myself and me - one
I am - the other
I could be.
The me is there
for all to see,
walking the treadmill,
grinding the way
laboriously.
Myself is a mystery
yet to unfold
hidden under
a comfort blanket
I'm told!

Expecting

Take me as you find me you're always welcome to call.

I might be in my gownie with my hair in a jumbly squall.

Depending on the time of day, breakfast dinner or tea,

you'll take me as you find me where chatting is totally free.

Take me as you find me I may be a little bit stressed.

I might be in a new dress all coiffed and pressed in my best.

Depending on the time of day, breakfast dinner or tea,

I'm simply waiting for Adventure to call, I wonder when it

will be.

Take me as you find me just rattle the letterbox do.

I might be waiting on tenterhooks I'm hoping it will be

You.

Depending on the time of day, breakfast dinner or tea,

just take me as you find me if I'm not on an adventurous

spree.

If you read my note you'll probably see I left the house

at half past three. My tote bag's filled with this and that,

a woolly scarf and my floppy hat, a nibbly biscuit, a flask of

tea, in fact everything for an emergency.

Please call back at another time, if you would be so kind,

I'm busy at the moment keeping that age thing out of mind!

Walking On

eggshells lie beneath

tentative feet

where steps so light on

tiptoes creep

with bated breath

lest with a crack or

careless word

the whole should shatter

and find themselves

ankle deep

in fiery volcanic matter

Words

I'm always writing words

writing words I sometimes can't explain.

They come from far away

drifting gently through my mind

interrupting my day because they will

be denied.

I tuck them quietly in a pocket

in the corner of my mind to

open in the peace of night.

Words that say so many things

to ponder and think about.

The way it is to feel, to see, to be free.

There is no time for an empty mind.

The quietest moment is never still

as words flow and flutter free like melodies.

Waiting for the X59

He crept to the front of the queue
brash and bold as if we wouldn't notice.
Interjected my conversation, I turned
to look was this a clever ploy or just
a chatty boy?

It's strange what people need to say
to share with no names either way.
He said he'd travelled the world
dressed in a vest tattoos on his
arms and chest.

He said he'd seen the world,
hair shaved pigtail like a feather
in his cap. I believed he'd seen
the world carried along with his
youthful surge.

Kilt swaying to the knees,

dull boots that grazed his crumpled

socks. I believed he'd seen those sunny

climes whilst serving cocktails to feed

the bread of sustenance.

His eyes of grey his leaner look told

stories from his adventure book.

One day he'd hang up his wandering

shoes and settle down but never

leave those youthful days.

He'd still smoke pot in a delightful

haze. Youth and freedom used in so

many different ways!

Out There

Oh yeah it's all out there

amongst the grime and grit

jostling crowds taken for

a ride the prices and rip offs

grabbing and greed it's all

out there.

Beneath the layers that

stream on the surface

of every street where people

meet and beggars creep

there's the genuine good

the smile that cares

hard working folk eager to

please happy to chat with

stories to tell.

Oh yeah it's all out there

Thank Goodness

Like Me

It's what people like me do
watching as the world
strides on by.
Catching the occasional eye
without recognition to them
I'm just a vision.

You'll find me in draughty corners
or settled on a seat too hard
for comfort.
Time passes by yet wishes it
could stay a while longer at any
time of day.

Nobody gets my drift or thinks
my thoughts as I shift stiffly
from my pew.
It's all in the mind you see the
then and now, the them and me

a story scribed by my pen!

Scrubbing the Cat

I looked at him in his raggedy state
as I scrubbed the kitchen floor.
He looked up at me as I shuffled the mop
he'd seen it all before.
I moved like a sprite and sung out of tune,
neither whisker nor tail gave a twitch.
He seemed quite relaxed, so tranquil
and cool, in fact hypnotised to the core.

Our glances met with half closed lids,
I knew that he instantly saw, I was
plotting and planning a devious move.
Would he fight tooth and nail or just claw?
'Why can't you be more like a horse
no rolling or messing about, just stand
on all fours and I'll groom you right down
a scrubbing's not only for floors.'

So I started to scrub him from head
down to tail, he purred as he arched up his back.
His head came up to meet the brush, his
eyes closed with pleasant rapport.
He looked brand new with a tail
held high as he skittered out of the door.
He ran straight past to do his best
and roll in the garden stour.

Now needless to say it's a scrub
every day 'cause he waits at the kitchen door!

So I'm Told.....

I've been told I knit with words

Slip one, knit one, drop one

Has a rhythm of its own

To merge, create a pattern

Either intricate or plain

Makes a foolish kind of imagery

As I'd just write about the holes!

Doubt

'Is that good enough?' she asked.

'I'm not so sure' was her reply.

Her brow wrinkled in a frown

as she pondered.

No matter what, the question

chose to ask again, each time

the answer unfulfilled

expressed a sigh.

'Is it ever good enough?'

The words with fearful dread,

a dervish dance spun and leapt

in a doubtful head.

Windows

Your eyes look down upon the scene
empty images reflect.

They blink not, squint not,
neither frown nor stare.
What secrets hold within?

Veiled in fine mist or heavy guise
give no story to your tale.

But as the moon lifts in the sky
to greet the sinking sun
your glow draws eyes like hungry moth –

as passers-by peep in

Weapon of choice

Clutched
in a crab like grip
poised
above a virgin page
suspended
the first thrill of stain in mark
or blot
takes time.

Keeper
of the means to flow
restrained
until descending
in a flurry becomes
an extension of thought
expresser of mind
a user of paper
in delightful frenzy
scratcher of words
teller of tales
scriber of scripts.

A valued weapon of choice
for those who take you up
hoping you will
ceaselessly
flow
to the end.

Welcome

So lovely to meet a deepest sleep
where slumber drifts beneath all
reality
where body nestles in softest folds
where breath is sweet and gently
flows from open lips.

So lovely to greet that deepest sleep
where all the world is calm at
peace
where troubles rest in an altered state
where sweet memories come
out to play.

Welcome to a deepest sleep
Waiting for your magic touch
Whatever time you choose
to take away the day.

Welcome!

Ode to a Long Marriage...

Do you think you could
Start the day in a better way?
A smile or a greeting would simply say,
"It's good to be here."

I don't mind giving you breakfast
in bed, but please it's the crumbs
so carelessly shed. They drift and shift
like sand on a beach to irritate places
now quite out of reach.

When I'm out for the day
my intention is clear. I hope you'll
make lunch with flamboyance, my dear.
But what is the point if you're set in
your ways. The oatmeal and spurtle
have seen better days.

You muddle along with no practical
spark, your methods leave me in awe.
They may suit *you* fine but don't make them
mine, I'm saying they're not without flaw.

Now when the day's done it's so peaceful in bed
'till I hear your sharp intake of breath.
Your swift turn of phrase sends me into a haze,
as you say those words that I dread.

"What's for dinner tomorrow?"
  Who says romance is dead?

Whispering

Listen to the silence. It loudly cries
and echoes on the air, to those who
hear beyond the innermost near.
That depth of something distant far beyond,
carrying to another realm.

Just listen to the silence deep and
quietly call. Transporting heart and soul to
timeless time. Where human echoes wanting
you to hear the call of quietness beckons
with no fear.

Whispering air that moves within this
sphere, is there to soothe and calm all inner
fear. So listen to the silence its presence
waiting still whispering.
So listen, hear!

Lost Words

Perhaps they fall on deaf ears
that do not let them in
or said in such a hurry
cascading carelessly without a thought.

Perhaps still nestling in the mind
no time to set them free
if left to drift and ponder
those words may never be!

Simplicity

I write but I'm not a poet

I paint but I'm not an artist

I breathe yet my breath is soft

I am me yet not myself

Who am I?

I wait with expectation.

ABOUT THE AUTHOR

I without words do not exist
I am invisible to you and myself
I am the inside looking out.
All the colours of this scene I absorb
and lock away to feed my soul.

The world does not know me, I am
too complex yet too uncomplicated,
a shell on the outside hides where
 nobody goes.
I tread with caution lest I capture me
escaping from that inner sanctuary.

I am accomplished in a human world
but don't look too closely you may see
nothing to please you.
Fear does not faze me, death does
not fear me, we walk together hand
in hand 'till one of us lets go.

As I age like a rusty bucket I will slowly
slip through the holes, my words will be
 confusing but I'll puzzle over them to
keep myself amused. I have cared too much,
loved too little, caution is my guardian,
watchful lest I elude it's craggy claws.

All I am saying is I am nothing
without these few simple words.

Thank You for reading this book.

I hope you may have found something

to touch you or entertain you.

Verba volant, scripta manent.

Best Wishes F.J.Milne

f.j.milnepoetry200@gmail.com

Printed in Great Britain
by Amazon